How To Buy A Fixer Upper

Turn your old home into a dream home

By Derrick Mitchell

Table of Contents

PROLOGUE

HOW DO YOU TURN A FIXER UPPER INTO YOUR DREAM HOME?

WHAT IS FHA?

QUICK OVERVIEW OF THE 203K PROCESS:

ELIGIBLE PROPERTIES FOR A 203K LOAN

FEATURES OF THE 203(K) LIMITED

TIMELINES, DISBURSEMENTS AND INSPECTIONS FOR THE 203(K)

203K HUD CONSULTANTS

LOOKING AT THE NUMBERS

RENOVATION SURVIVAL GUIDE

SURVIVING THE CONTRACTORS

SURVIVING THE CONSTRUCTION ZONE

POTENTIAL HOME CHECKLIST

RENOVATION CHECKLIST

HERE ARE SOME REAL-LIFE SUCCESS STORIES OF 203K LOANS

Prologue

After years of renting apartments, my wife and I decided that it was time to buy a home. On the weekends, we would drive around town looking at new homes. The newer homes were very nice, but we just couldn't find a home that fit all of our needs. Our luck changed one day when we came across an older home that was in a perfect location and it had everything that my wife and I wanted in a dream home (cul-de-sac, ideal school zone, privacy, more land, larger space, and character), but there was a problem: our "dream home" needed updating and we had no money for renovations! But with a lot of trial and error and research, we were able to find a solution! Keep reading, it gets good...

Unless you have an unlimited budget, just about any home you buy will require compromise. The house that's move-in ready might have fewer bedrooms than you'd like. The house that's in the perfect location might need a lot of repairs. Sometimes it feels like you'll never be able to afford the house you truly want. This is where the **FHA 203(k)** loan can be a huge help. By using the 203k loan, my wife and I were able to buy a fixer upper and turn it into our dream home just like they do on one of our favorite TV shows "Fixer Upper". I want to show others how they can do the same! Let's talk about this loan for a second.

How do you turn a fixer upper into your dream home?

Well…The answer to the question above is – **the FHA 203(k) Loan!**

The purchase of a house that needs repair is often a difficult solution, because the bank won't lend the money to buy the house until the repairs are complete, and the repairs can't be done until the house has been purchased.

HUD's 203(k) program can help you with the purchase or refinance of a property by allowing you to roll-in the costs of repairs and improvements up to 110% of the after improved value of the home with a minimum 3.5% down payment.

I hope you find the following pages below helpful. You will find information about the 203K loan and personal experiences that my wife and I went through on our "Fixer Upper" Journey. Also, there will be "golden nuggets" throughout the eBook; really pay attention to those. Ok let's get started!

What is FHA?

FHA 203K

BUY IT - FIX IT- ALL IN ONE LOAN

The Federal Housing Administration (FHA), which is part of the Department of Housing and Urban Development (HUD), administers various single family mortgage insurance programs. The Section 203(k) program is HUD's primary program for the rehabilitation and repair of single family properties. As such, it is an important tool for community and neighborhood revitalization and for expanding homeownership opportunities.

203(k) - How Is It Different From Other Loans?

An FHA 203(k) rehab loan, also referred to as a renovation loan, enables homebuyers and homeowners to finance both the purchase or refinance along with the renovation of a home through a **single mortgage**. Instead of applying for multiple loans, an FHA 203(k) rehab loan allows homebuyers to purchase or refinance their primary home and renovate it with one convenient loan. This allows the buyer to finance the cost of improvements into the purchase or refinance of a home.

When a homebuyer wants to purchase a house in need of repair or modernization, the homebuyer usually has to obtain financing first to purchase the dwelling; additional financing to do the rehabilitation construction; and a permanent mortgage when the work is completed to pay off the interim loans with a permanent mortgage. Often the interim financing (the acquisition and construction loans) involves relatively high interest rates and short amortization periods. The Section 203(k) program was designed to address this situation. **The borrower can get just one mortgage loan, at a long-term fixed (or adjustable) rate, to finance both the acquisition and the rehabilitation of the property**. To provide funds for the rehabilitation, the mortgage amount is based on the projected value of the property with the work completed, taking into account the cost of the work.

There are two Different 203(k) Loans

Picking which loan suits you best will rely upon the amount of improvement your property needs.

Limited 203k Loan: The 203(k) "Limited" is an all-in-one loan used for homes that need minor repairs. It allows borrowers to finance the purchase of an existing home and make improvements or upgrades up to **$35,000 before move-in**. There are no minimum repair costs and the borrower must occupy the property.

The 203k Standard Loan: The Standard 203(k) is an all-in-one loan used when homes need major rehabilitation, or when repairs are structural, involves landscaping, or when the renovation costs **exceed $35,000**. There must be a minimum of $5,000 worth of repairs, and again, the borrower must occupy the property. FHA loan limits are based on property type and location of the property being financed. A portion of the loan proceeds are used to pay the seller, or, if a refinance, to pay off the existing mortgage, and the remaining funds are placed in an escrow account and released as rehabilitation is completed. You may also roll in up to six months of mortgage payments the HUD consultant determines you need to be displaced from the home during the repairs.

Here is a chart that shows you the difference between both 203(k) loans.

PROGRAM GUIDELINE	203(K) LIMITED	203(K) STANDARD
Down Payment & Credit Underwriting	The same as for any loan.	The same as for any loan.
Who can get a 203(K)?	Owner-occupant borrowers, HUD approved non profits, government agencies.	The same as for any loan.
Eligible Improvements	No minimum repair requirement. Up to $35,000 of minor repair. Cannot be used for structural repairs.	A minimum $5,000 requirement for improvements. Any repair is acceptable, however – health and safety items and building code or ordinance violations must be addressed first. Then, minor repairs and discretionary items may be included.
203(k) Consultant	203(k) consultant is not required.	203(k) consultant is used.
What may be included in rehabilitation cost?	Total cost of rehabilitation (including energy package and lead-based paint abatement costs,) contingency reserves, inspections (if required), supplemental origination fee and discount points, all not exceed $35,000.	The total cost of rehabilitation (including energy package and lead based paint abatement costs, consultant fees, and architectural and engineering fees) contingency reserves, inspections, up to 6 months PITI, and supplemental origination fee. The loan amount including the cost of rehabilitation cannot exceed the FHA maximum loan limit for jurisdiction.
Contingency Reserves	A contingency reserve is not required. Lenders have the option to establish a reserve.	The lender must establish a contingency reserve when the property is 30 years or older. The reserve should be between 10 and 20 percent of the rehabilitation cost, depending on the complexity of the project.
Contractors	Contractors provide written work plan and cost estimates. Contractors must be licensed and bonded, as required locality.	203(k) consultant provides a work write-up including a cost estimate and work plan. Borrower selects contractors with assistance of the consultant and review by the lender.
Allowable Fees	Supplemental origination fee of 1.50% of the rehabilitation costs or $300, whichever is greater, plus inspection fees, and title update fees.	Same as Limited 203(k) plus financed mortgage payments, and architectural and engineering fees.

We will discuss both loans in detail, but first let's discuss the 203(k) process from start to finish.

Quick Overview of the 203k Process:

1. If you are purchasing or refinancing a home – step one is to get pre-approved by your lender

Many home buyers may rush out to look at properties before speaking with a qualified Renovation Loan Specialist, which obviously may present some future challenges after a purchase contract has been accepted by a seller.

You will need to select an FHA-approved 203K Lender. Not every mortgage lender originates 203(k) loans, so to save time you can **Click** HERE to search for lenders who can originate 203k loans near you. Once you have talked to a lender and received your pre-approval, you can start the house hunting and Preliminary Market Analysis.

2. Preliminary Market Analysis

Now it's time to find a house! With your loan **pre-qualification letter** stating the terms and a maximum loan amount that fits your budget, it is time to start searching for properties with your real estate agent.

Once you've found a potential property, you need to have a **preliminary market analysis** completed. This is spelling out the rehab work, rough estimated cost of renovation, and estimated market value of the property upon completion of renovation. This should be performed prior to signing the sales contract and before you commit funds for an **appraisal**.

The market analysis should include:

- The extent of the rehabilitation work required (Contact a 203K Consultant/Contractor)
- The rough cost estimate of the work (Contact a 203K Consultant or/and Contractor)
- The expected market value of the property after completion of the work (Real Estate Agent)

 Contact a licensed contractor to do a free renovation estimate.

3. Writing the Sales Contract

Once the preliminary market analysis is complete, an offer to the seller should be drawn up. *Your agent will handle this part!* A provision should be included in the sales contract that the buyer has applied for FHA 203k financing, and that the contract is contingent upon loan approval which can take up to **45 days to close** and the buyer's acceptance of additional required improvements as determined by HUD, the Appraiser and/or the Rehab Lender. Once accepted you will need to contact your Lender to get the 203K paper work rolling.

4. Contractor Bids, Work Write-up, Cost Estimate and HUD Case

With the **203K Consultants** help, a feasibility study and preliminary cost estimate is used to produce the SOR – Specification of Repairs. After having refined and determined the specification of repairs, the Contractor submits the bid for repairs.

📙 I suggest that you choose a Contractor that has experience working with 203(k) loans. Make sure you're going with reputable contractors.

The way to determine which contractors are going to be able to participate in FHA 203k loans is by:

1. Contacting them personally

2. Go over the premise of the loan

3. Make sure they understand how it works

4. Taking the time to go through their financials—making sure that they have the means and knowledge to be able to participate in a loan like this.

For contractors, if they can't float the loan or, "float the job," as some would say, then they're not going to be able to participate in FHA 203k loans. Essentially, "floating the job," means being able to **finance the job** right from the start. With a Full 203k loan, contractors don't receive any upfront cash. So, it's important for contractors to understand this all up front. Your loan officer will help you determine if your Contractor is qualified to do a 203K loan.

The following pages are copies of my actual Contractor Bid and 203K Consultant Write Up for my 203k Loan.

Example Contractor Bid:

General Contractor

September 13, 2017

The following is a breakdown for the proposed work on your new home:

Kitchen

1) Remove existing cabinets, appliances and two walls.
Note: Wall removal includes leaving columns as applicable, relocating electrical outlets and switches
2) Install custom cabinets to include soft close doors and drawers. Bump area where sink is located into the living room approx. 24". Relocate plumbing for sink as required. Install cabinets under bay window with pull out drawers.
3) Install granite counter tops with under mount sink.
4) Vent microwave through back wall.
5) Set appliances (customer to provide appliances and faucet)

Total = $26,000
Labor to remove cabinets = $500
Labor for wall removal and completion = $2,800
Labor for electrical and plumbing = 1,800
Materials for cabinets = $15,000
Materials for countertops = $4,200
Labor to set appliances = $750
Labor to vent microwave - $950

Staircase

1) Open wall between foyer and hallway as much as possible.
2) Install hardwood on steps.
3) Install new rails, spindles, grab bars on each side

Total = $8,400
Labor for steps = $3,750
Labor for wall rebuild = $1,500
Materials for steps = $1,500
Materials for rails = $1,650

Entrance into Office

1) Remove two columns. Frame in half round and drywall.
2) Install interior French doors, trim out and paint

Total = $2,500

Example Contractor Bid Continued:

General Contractor

Labor for general construction = $1,800
Materials = $700

Flooring downstairs

1) Remove existing hardwood and shoe molding
2) Install new hardwood in entire downstairs (Water resistant materials)
3) Remove/reset commode when applicable

Total = $8,400
Labor = $5,450
Materials = $2,800
Plumbing for commode = $150

**Note: Fireplace requirements still need to be discussed.

Grand Total = $46,700

Terms - TBD

Warranty - Two years on all workmanship

Example 203K Consultant Write Up:

MITCHELL RENOVATION AT ▮▮▮▮▮

Inspection Date: 10/04/2017   **Consultant:** ▮▮▮▮▮   **Contractor:** ▮▮▮▮▮

Applicant:
DERRICK MITCHELL
▮▮▮▮▮

Property Address:
▮▮▮▮▮

Lender:
▮▮▮▮▮

The following is the scope of work (Work Write Up WWU) document that represents the agreed upon items to be included in the escrow account for the rehabilitation loan to be obtained by the above indicated borrowers. This document (also known as the Specification of Repairs or SOR) has been created in most cases using the information and estimates of a selected contractor's bid.

Borrower acknowledges that this WWU was created based upon limited access to the property and it's systems or components. Changes are to be expected once work has begun. Borrower agrees to hold the consultant harmless for any changes, latent or concealed defects that may be identified following the close of escrow. Borrower further agrees to bring to the attention of the consultant (in writing) all suggested changes as identified by the contractor or that they themselves would like to have completed using the funds from the escrow account prior to the change order item work begins. Borrower and contractor agree that any work performed outside the scope of the WWU without prior written approval from the consultant/lender, may not be paid by the escrow funds. Contractor will provide a written Change Order Invoice to the borrower for review and signed acceptance. This executed Change Order Invoice will then be submitted to the consultant for review and submission to the Lender for PRIOR Approval. Should the change order include Desired (not safety or soundness required repairs), it may be suggested that the contractor establish separate payment arrangements and terms as paymentfor desired changes will not be disbursed until at least 80% of the listed items on the WWU have been disbursed. In most cases, this means the payment for these desired changes will not be disbursed until the final draw request.

Should the borrower be using the 203k FHA Rehab Loan, this WWU will report next to each line item a classification for the repair of M- Mandatory, R-Recommended by Consultant/Contractor, and D-Desired by borrower. This is important to note as should significant changes to the scope of work be identified after the close of escrow, the consultant may instruct the contractor to complete only those items identified with the classification of M. Funds allocated for items classified as R or D may be re-directed as necessary to correct any newly identified safety and/or soundness concerns as the FHA 203k Loan program dictates all Safety/Soundness repairs must be completed.

Borrower and Contractor agree to mutual and frequent communication during the project and all parties will make every effort to attend all inspections as required for the terms of the loan for which this WWU has been created.

Borrower and Contractor future agree that their contractual relationship may be terminated by either party with a minimum of a 10 day written notice (as verified by a signed return receipt for the delivery of such notice). Other terms and condition for this termination of contract may be required by the specific lending institution. All parties by their signature agree to be mindful of these terms as needed prior to close of escrow of the loan.

Borrower has agreed prior to the creation of the WWU to a Homeowner/Consultant Agreement. The terms of that agreement are binding throughout the Pre-Closing period as well as the entire duration of the consultant's activities during the rehabilitation and construction process.

Example Consultant Write Up Continued:

Construction Categories, Items & Costs (Construction Cost Estimate)

16. Doors (Int.)

Material: $500.00 | Tax: $0.00 | Labor: $500.00 | Total: $1000.00

Repair Item	Repair Class	M.Unit	M.Qty	M.Cost	M.Tax	L.Unit	L.Qty	L.Cost	Sub Total
1 Install interior door .. **Location:** Living Room **Repairer:** Contractor .. Repair Notes: INCLUDES: INTERIOR FRENCH DOORS, TRIM OUT, AND PAINTING	D	EA	1	500.00	0.00	EA	1	500.00	1000.00
16. Doors (Int.) Totals:				500.00	0.00			500.00	1000.00

Category Details

17. Partition Wall

Material: $1500.00 | Tax: $0.00 | Labor: $4300.00 | Total: $5800.00

Repair Item	Repair Class	M.Unit	M.Qty	M.Cost	M.Tax	L.Unit	L.Qty	L.Cost	Sub Total
1 Modify Walls .. **Location:** Kitchen **Repairer:** Contractor .. Repair Notes: REMOVE EXISTING WALL AND REPLACE INTERIOR KITCHEN WALL WITH COLUMNS	D	LS	1	800.00	0.00	LS	1	2000.00	2800.00
2 Modify Walls .. **Location:** Hallway **Repairer:** Contractor .. Repair Notes: OPEN AND REBUILD WALL BETWEEN FOYER AND HALLWAY AS MUCH AS POSSIBLE.	D	LS	1	400.00	0.00	LS	1	1100.00	1500.00
3 Modify Walls .. **Location:** Living Room **Repairer:** Contractor .. Repair Notes: INCLUDES: REMOVING TWO COLUMNS, FRAME IN HALF ROUND, AND DRYWALL.	D	LS	1	300.00	0.00	LS	1	1200.00	1500.00
17. Partition Wall Totals:				1500.00	0.00			4300.00	5800.00

Category Details

18. Plaster/Drywall

Material: $200.00 | Tax: $0.00 | Labor: $400.00 | Total: $600.00

Repair Item	Repair Class	M.Unit	M.Qty	M.Cost	M.Tax	L.Unit	L.Qty	L.Cost	Sub Total
1 Drywall mud & tape .. **Location:** 1st Floor **Repairer:** Contractor	D	LS	1	200.00	0.00	LS	1	400.00	600.00
18. Plaster/Drywall Totals:				200.00	0.00			400.00	600.00

19. Decorating

Material: $200.00 | Tax: $0.00 | Labor: $600.00 | Total: $800.00

Repair Item	Repair Class	M.Unit	M.Qty	M.Cost	M.Tax	L.Unit	L.Qty	L.Cost	Sub Total
1 PREP & PAINT .. **Location:** 1st Floor **Repairer:** Contractor	D	LS	1	200.00	0.00	LS	1	600.00	800.00
19. Decorating Totals:				200.00	0.00			600.00	800.00

Category Details

21. Stairs

Material: $3150.00 | Tax: $0.00 | Labor: $3750.00 | Total: $6900.00

Repair Item	Repair Class	M.Unit	M.Qty	M.Cost	M.Tax	L.Unit	L.Qty	L.Cost	Sub Total
1 INSTALL OAK STEPS, TREADS, AND KICKS .. **Location:** Hallway **Repairer:** Contractor	D	LS	1	1500.00	0.00	LS	1	3750.00	5250.00
2 INSTALL HAND RAILING AND BALUSTERS .. **Location:** Kitchen **Repairer:** Contractor	D	LS	1	1650.00	0.00	LS	1	0.00	1650.00
21. Stairs Totals:				3150.00	0.00			3750.00	6900.00

Category Details

23. Wood Floors

Material: $2800.00 | Tax: $0.00 | Labor: $5450.00 | Total: $8250.00

Repair Item	Repair Class	M.Unit	M.Qty	M.Cost	M.Tax	L.Unit	L.Qty	L.Cost	Sub Total
1 Install new hardwood floors. .. **Location:** 1st Floor **Repairer:** Contractor .. Repair Notes: INCLUDES: REMOVAL OF EXISTING HARDWOOD AND SHOE MOLDING, NEW HARDWOOD IN ENTIRE DOWNSTAIRS (WATER RESISTANT MATERIALS)	D	LS	1	2800.00	0.00	LS	1	5450.00	8250.00
23. Wood Floors Totals:				2800.00	0.00			5450.00	8250.00

Example Consultant Write Up Continued:

Category Details

27. Plumbing

| | | Material: $230.00 | Tax: $0.00 | Labor: $920.00 | Total: $1150.00 |

Repair Item	Repair Class	M.Unit	M.Qty	M.Cost	M.Tax	L.Unit	L.Qty	L.Cost	Sub Total
1 Plumbing : other ... **Location:** Kitchen **Repairer:** Contractor ... *Repair Notes:* INCLUDES RELOCATE PLUMBING FOR SINK TO BUMP AREA WHERE SINK IS LOCATED INTO THE LIVING ROOM APPRA 24"	D	LS	1	200.00	0.00	LS	1	800.00	1000.00
2 Plumbing / fixtures ... **Location:** 1st Floor **Repairer:** Contractor ... *Repair Notes:* REMOVAL AND REINSTALL COMMODE, ETC. FOR NEW HARDWOOD	D	LS	1	30.00	0.00	LS	1	120.00	150.00

27. Plumbing Totals: 230.00 0.00 920.00 1150.00

Category Details

28. Electrical

| | | Material: $300.00 | Tax: $0.00 | Labor: $500.00 | Total: $800.00 |

Repair Item	Repair Class	M.Unit	M.Qty	M.Cost	M.Tax	L.Unit	L.Qty	L.Cost	Sub Total
1 Electrical ... **Location:** Kitchen **Repairer:** Contractor ... *Repair Notes:* INCLUDES REMOVAL AND RELOCATION OF EXISTING SWITCHES AND OUTLETS	D	LS	1	300.00	0.00	LS	1	500.00	800.00

28. Electrical Totals: 300.00 0.00 500.00 800.00

Category Details

31. Cabinetry

| | | Material: $18800.00 | Tax: $0.00 | Labor: $900.00 | Total: $19700.00 |

Repair Item	Repair Class	M.Unit	M.Qty	M.Cost	M.Tax	L.Unit	L.Qty	L.Cost	Sub Total
1 Install new base and wall cabinets ... **Location:** Kitchen **Repairer:** Contractor ... *Repair Notes:* INCLUDES REMOVAL OF EXISTING CABINETS AND COUNTER TOPS. SOFT CLOSE DOORS AND PULL OUT DRAWERS. CABINETS UNDER BAY WINDOW	D	LS	1	15000.00	0.00	LS	1	500.00	15500.00
2 Install Counter Tops ... **Location:** Kitchen **Repairer:** Contractor ... *Repair Notes:* GRANITE TOPS WITH UNDER MOUNT SINK	D	LS	1	3800.00	0.00	LS	1	400.00	4200.00

31. Cabinetry Totals: 18800.00 0.00 900.00 19700.00

Category Details

32. Appliances

| | | Material: $5200.00 | Tax: $0.00 | Labor: $1500.00 | Total: $6700.00 |

Repair Item	Repair Class	M.Unit	M.Qty	M.Cost	M.Tax	L.Unit	L.Qty	L.Cost	Sub Total
1 Hood Fan/Light ... **Location:** Kitchen **Repairer:** Contractor ... *Repair Notes:* INSTALL HOOD VENT THRU BACK WALL	D	EA	1	200.00	0.00	EA	1	750.00	950.00
2 INSTALL APPLIANCE PACKAGE ... **Location:** Kitchen **Repairer:** Contractor	D	LS	1	5000.00	0.00	LS	1	750.00	5750.00

32. Appliances Totals: 5200.00 0.00 1500.00 6700.00

Category Details

Example Consultant Write Up Continued:

Project Construction and Fee Estimate
MITCHELL RENOVATION AT ▉▉▉▉▉▉▉

Construction Categories		Total $
Section 1	Masonry	0.00
Section 2	Siding	0.00
Section 3	Gutters/Downspouts	0.00
Section 4	Roof	0.00
Section 5	Shutters	0.00
Section 6	Exteriors	0.00
Section 7	Walks	0.00
Section 8	Driveways	0.00
Section 9	Painting (Ext.)	0.00
Section 10	Caulking	0.00
Section 11	Fencing	0.00
Section 12	Grading/Landscaping	0.00
Section 13	Windows	0.00
Section 14	Weatherstrip	0.00
Section 15	Doors (Ext.)	0.00
Section 16	Doors (Int.)	1000.00
Section 17	Partition Wall	5800.00
Section 18	Plaster/Drywall	600.00
Section 19	Decorating	800.00
Section 20	Wood Trim	0.00
Section 21	Stairs	6900.00
Section 22	Closets	0.00
Section 23	Wood Floors	8250.00
Section 24	Finished Floors	0.00
Section 25	Ceramic Tile	0.00
Section 26	Bath Accessories	0.00
Section 27	Plumbing	1150.00
Section 28	Electrical	800.00
Section 29	Heating	0.00
Section 30	Insulation	0.00
Section 31	Cabinetry	19700.00
Section 32	Appliances	6700.00
Section 33	Basements	0.00
Section 34	Cleanup	0.00
Section 35	Miscellaneous	0.00
Section 1 - 35 Construction Cost SUBTOTAL		$51700.00

Fee Name	Fee Details	Total $
Draw Fees	3 Draws at 200.000	600.00
TOTAL	Fee Grand Total	$ 600.00

Sub Total Name	Notes	GRAND Total
Construction Subtotal		$51700.00
Contingency Amount	10%	$5170.00
Fee Total	Fee Grand Total	$ 600.00
	Grand Total	$ 57,470.00

After the Lender receives the bid from the Contractor and a write up from your 203K Consultant, they will request the HUD case number and the project will now move quickly to the appraisal stage.

Note: **HUD does not require a Consultant on a Limited 203k loan** (a rehab with minor repairs that total less than $35,000 and/or that does not include structural repairs). However, the experience and value of the consultant's advice can often save more than the fees charged for the service.

 Your lender will typically provide a 203K Consultant for you, if not, just ask them.

5. Lender Prepares/Issues Firm Commitment Application

After the appraisal and the contractor's bid have been accepted, the lender will issue a Conditional Commitment and Statement of Appraised Value to establish the maximum insurable mortgage amount for the property.

6. Mortgage Loan Closing

It usually takes 45-60 days to close on a 203K loan, which is longer than a regular home loan, but once you reach the closing table the process will be just like a typical closing. The buyer and seller will sign final loan documents and the close of escrow date is met. The lender will prepare the Loan agreement and other pre-closing documents required for the mortgage closing. The Agreement is executed by both borrower and the lender, and establishes conditions under which the lender will release funds from the Rehab Escrow Account.

A few of these conditions include the construction draw schedule, fees schedule, work item change orders and identity of interest statement.

7. Construction Begins

At closing, mortgage proceeds are disbursed, and the Renovation Escrow Account is established. **Construction may begin immediately and must begin within 30 days of closing.**

Contact your Contractor and 203k Consultant ASAP and let them know that they now have a green light to proceed with the renovation!

8. Funds are Released from Escrow Account

Funds are disbursed to the General Contractor according to the Renovation Loan Agreement. Changes to the work write-up are made through written change orders and are typically inspected by the Consultant or Lender's Fee Inspector. **To ensure completion of the job, ten percent of each draw is held back**; this money is paid after the lender determines there will be no liens on the property. A final release of the funds confirms the substantial competition of the renovations.

Now let's look inside the 203K loan a bit deeper.

Eligible Properties For a 203K Loan

There are a few types of properties that are eligible for 203k loans and there are some that do not qualify. For example, investment properties that you purchase to make profits do not qualify when applying for this type of loan, but for investors there are a few work arounds (See Golden Nuggets below).

There is a loan available for investors called the HomeStyle Loan. This loan is designed to allow investors to participate in renovation lending versus FHA 203K because you don't have to live in the property. Buyers and investors can use the HomeStyle loan to purchase and renovate vacation homes that can be rented out.

An investor can still use a 203k loan but there's only one caveat: the borrower must live in the property for at least twelve months. You can say that the 203K loan is like the entry loan to becoming a property investor because FHA requires you to live in the home for a year, but then it can be turned into a rental or sold for a return, and you can then move on to another property. This is a great way to get your feet wet in the real estate investment game.

Eligible

- One to two unit properties
- Manufactured housing (singlewide, doublewide, and triplewide)
- The rehab must not impact the structural components of the structure and must comply with all other requirements for manufactured homes.
- FHA approved condominiums and site condos
  The rehab and improvements are limited to the interior of the unit, except for the installation of firewalls in the attic of the unit
- HUD REO property
  The property must be identified as eligible for 203k financing as evidenced on the sales contract or addendum

Ineligible

- Demolished homes
- Raised homes
- Structures relocated to/from another location
- Mixed-use properties
- Co-ops
- Non-FHA approved condos
- Investment properties
- Mobile homes

Note: Homes that haven't been completed are not allowed on the FHA 203k loan; construction of the property must have been completed for at least one year. Evidence of completion would be a Certificate of Occupancy or other similar documentation from local municipality.

A 203(k) mortgage may be originated on a "mixed use" residential property provided:

1. The property has no greater than twenty five percent for a one story building; thirty three percent for a three story building; and forty nine percent for a two story building, of its floor area used for commercial (storefront) purposes.

2. The commercial use will not affect the health and safety of the occupants of the residential property.

3. The rehabilitation funds will only be used for the residential functions of the dwelling and areas used to access the residential part of the property.

A 203(k) mortgage may be originated on a condominium provided:

1. The condominium project has been approved by FHA

2. Must be owner occupied (no investors)

3. Rehab is limited only to the interior of the property

4. The lesser of five units in the project or twenty five percent of the total number of units can be undergoing rehabilitation at the same time

5. The maximum amount of the loan cannot exceed one hundred percent of the after improved value

6. No more than four condo units per building

How the Program Can Be Used

This program can be used to accomplish rehabilitation and/or improvement of an existing one-to-four unit dwelling in one of three ways:

1. To purchase a home and rehabilitate it.
2. To purchase a dwelling on another site, move it onto a new foundation and rehabilitate it.
3. To refinance an existing mortgage and rehabilitate the home.

Now let's look at the Features of a the 203k Loans.

Features of the 203(k) Limited

Eligible and Ineligible Improvements for the 203(k) LIMITED

Eligible Improvements include:

203(k) Limited loan is intended to facilitate uncomplicated rehabilitation and/or improvements to a home.

- Repair/Replacement of roofs, gutters and downspouts
- Repair/Replacement/upgrade of existing HVAC systems
- Repair/Replacement/upgrade of plumbing and electrical systems
- Repair/Replacement of flooring
- Minor renovation, such as kitchens & baths, which do not involve structural repairs
- Painting, both exterior and interior
- Weatherization, including storms windows and doors, insulation, weather stripping, etc.
- Purchase and installation of appliances, including free-standing ranges, refrigerators, washers/dryers, dishwashers and microwave ovens
- Septic system and/or well repair or replacement
- Accessibility improvements for persons with disabilities
- Lead-based paint stabilization or abatement of lead-based paint hazards
- Repair/replace/add exterior decks, patios, porches
- Basement finishing and renovation with does not involve structural repairs
- Basement waterproofing
- Window and door replacements and exterior wall re-siding

Ineligible Improvements include:

- Renovation involving structural changes, like moving a load-bearing wall, or new construction, like adding rooms
- Landscaping or Fencing
- Work that will not start within 30 days of loan closing or will cause the borrower to be displaced from the home for more than 30 days or renovations that will take more than 6 months to complete
- Luxury items like swimming pools, hot tubs, tennis courts, etc.

Features of the 203(k) Full

Eligible and Ineligible Improvements for the 203(k) Standard Loan

Eligible:

- Full kitchen or bathroom remodel
- Garage (attached/detached/new)
- Structural alterations and additions
- Major Landscaping/decks/fencing
- Permanent improvements to the house
- Install appliances
- Repair swimming pool
- Install flooring / tile
- Interior and exterior painting
- Improvements that are a permanent part of the real estate

Ineligible:

- New tennis court
- Gazebo or bathhouse
- Additions or alterations for commercial use
- Photo mural
- New Swimming pool
- Outdoor fireplace / barbecue pit
- Other types of luxury items

Contractor Requirements

Borrowers must use contractors to complete rehab unless borrower can provide documente proof that they can perform the work. Example: Borrower is a licensed plumber or electrician, etc.

Timelines, Disbursements and Inspections for the 203(k)

Timeline

When the loan closes, the mortgage proceeds will be disbursed to pay off the seller of the existing property and the Rehabilitation Escrow Account will be established. Construction may begin. **The homeowner has up to six months to complete the work depending on the extent of work to be completed.** Borrowers can request time extensions if the work exceeds six months.

Borrowers can request time extensions if the work exceeds six months. The extension paperwork needs be signed by the borrower, contractor, and the consultant then submitted to the lender for approval. The paper work must include all work that hasn't been done, along with an estimated time of completion. Once approved the lender will extend the life of your 203k loan so that the work can be completed.

Disbursements

As construction progresses, funds are released after the work is inspected by a HUD-approved inspector. **A maximum of five draws are allowed. Draw amounts may vary and are based on the work performed.** Disbursements are made as each phase of the project is completed based on the draw paperwork provided by the consultant. Inspections are required prior to each disbursement.

A ten percent **holdback** is required on each draw released from the Rehabilitation Escrow Account. The Holdback/Contingency Fee is:

1) Used as an incentive to insure all work is completed and to cover health, safety and unplanned issues that arise during construction.

2) Required on FHA 203(k) Full; recommended on Limited loan

3) Required on properties older than thirty years and/or over $7,500 in rehabilitation costs.

4) A minimum of ten percent of the cost or rehabilitation and maximum of twenty percent.

There is a ten to twenty percent **Contingency Reserve** (which is an amount that's added to the renovation escrow to allow for unanticipated cost overruns). You can use these reserves to add or make changes to the original work right up or budget. For example, we used our contingency reserves to add additional recess lighting in our kitchen and a transom above our office doors.

If not used (after all construction is complete) the remaining amount from the holdbacks and contingency reserves will be applied to pay down the principal balance of the loan. The total of all holdbacks may be released only after a final inspection of the rehabilitation and issuance of the Final Release Notice.

203k Hud Consultants

What exactly are the services provided by the 203k Consultant? Here's an overview:

The role of a 203k consultant is to meet with the borrower and prepare applicable reports for the lender in connection with the property and renovation project.

The consultant will prepare a feasibility study, inspect the property, identify all required architectural exhibits (well/septic certificates, termite reports, etc.), inspect the work for completion and quality of workmanship at each draw request.

- **Home Inspections**: The first step for the HUD 203k Consultant is a property inspection. First identifying the repairs that must be made to meet the HUD Minimum Code Standards. At the same time, the consultant will also review other desired improvements with the homeowner and gather necessary information to detail these improvements in the final work write-up.

- **Work Write-Up**: The final work write-up identifies in detail the complete scope of work. Each work item will also be shown with an estimated cost. This cost breakdown helps you evaluate how your desired improvements relate to your anticipated renovation budget. **At this point, it's often advisable to review your wish list of desired improvements, do some additional prioritizing and make adjustments to your scope of work to stay within your budget.**

- **Draw Inspections** – The lender will often hire the HUD Consultant to provide the additional service of making site inspections prior to the payment of each draw request. The Consultant will inspect the amount of work completed, reconcile the completed work to the contract bids, and approve the release of funds from the renovation escrow to be paid to the contractor.

- If there are changes to the original plans the consultant will review the proposed changes to the work write-up and prepare a change of order, if applicable. The 203k consultant will also inform the lender of the progress of the rehabilitation and any problem that arise.

So how much do these services cost? FHA has established a schedule of allowable fees to be charged by HUD Consultants. Discuss with you Lender. See the chart below.

203K Consultant Fees	
Renovation Amount	Consultant Fee
Up to $7,500	$400
$7,501 - $15,000	$500
$15,001 - $30,000	$600
$30,001 - $50,000	$700
$50,001 - $75,000	$800
$75,000 - $100,000	$900
More than $100,000	$1,000
Other Fees	
Feasibility Study	$100 - $200
Draw Inspection	$50 - $200

Looking at the Numbers

Below are **examples** of how the dollars and cents break down typically for both 203k loan types. Keep in mind this is simply intended to provide an overview and calculations can be **different for your loan**.

203(k) Standard Basic Costs	
Purchase Price	$200,000
Rehab work	$50,000
Overall 30-year fixed-rate mortgage (less 3.5% down payment of $8,750)	$241,250
Mortgage rate: (Estimated % could be lower) (based on HUD estimate that rates average 1% more than standard FHA rates, currently 5%)	6%
Closing costs, upfront insurance premium, etc. (see additional fees)	$7,221
FHA annual insurance fee (55 basis points of the outstanding loan balance)	$1,366 ($114 in monthly installments)
Monthly Payment	$1,604
Additional Fees	
The write-up fees and other charges may be rolled into the rehabilitation portion of the loan. The closing cost and the up-front insurance premium can be included in the loan as well. Standard (k) borrowers can also roll in monthly payments of the mortgage until the property is livable (up to six months).	
Up-front FHA mortgage insurance premium	1.75% $4,221
Consultant initial architectural draft	$500
Charges for signing off on work draws	$250 ($50, up to five inspections)
Supplemental origination fee (allowed on 203(k) loans by HUD – 1.5% of rehabilitation portion of loan)	$750
Closing cost (estimate)	$1,500
Total fees	$7,221
Loan-to-Value	
Purchase and rehabilitation costs	$241,250
Fees	$7,221
Total	$248,471
"As -improved" value	$250,000
Loan to Value	99.4%

203(k) Limited Cost Example	
Purchase Price ("As-Is" Appraisal Value)	$250,000
Renovation Material Labor Costs (detailed bids in hand)	$32,000
Other Allowable Costs (permits, inspections, etc)	$2,000
Supplemental Origination Fee (1.5% or $350)	$510
Total Renovation Costs	$34,510
Total Purchase and Renovation	$284,510
"After-Improved" Appraisal Value ("subject-to renovation)	$300,000
Lesser of: "After-improved" Appraisal Value x 110% Or "As-is" Appraisal Value + Renovation Costs	$284,510
Maximum Loan Amount (96.5% of above)	$274,552

So, there you have an example of real-world numbers. I hope this is helpful in bringing the various steps together from a financial perspective, and I hope this added a little extra fun if you enjoy crunching numbers. Now let's discuss how to survive during your renovations. Renovating a home can have some challenges but the following guides will help you tremendously on your 203K journey!

Renovation Survival Guide

Here are some suggested steps to prepare yourself for renovation success:

1) Schedule a family meeting. Get the whole family and discuss the impact that the renovations will have on the day to day activities. Make sure that everyone recognizes that this is going to be challenging. The message is that if we work together, if we anticipate and plan ahead, we can survive. I encourage you to run through this list and discuss each point as a group.

2) Understand the remodels may take longer than you'd like. There will be obstructions that will show up that will affect your completion date. Simply know this upfront.

3) Expect things to go wrong. This is part of the renovation game, so realize that there's no good to come from getting frustrated or angry over these setbacks, there's only stress to come from worrying about things that you can't control.

4) Anticipate issues and postponements. A remodeling venture never appears to go as easily as we'd like. When you have your home loaded with temporary workers and everything is torn up around you, it will change the way that you live. You may reach a point where you believe you can't manage the burdens any more. Then take a full breath and understand that soon you'll be thinking back on this experience and it won't have the capacity to hurt you any longer. Think about the end goal and your delightful home!

5) Life must go on. Obviously, you'll need to make some life adjustments, but you're not going to put your whole life on hold. You may need to go to work, children may need to go to school and other basic things need to occur. For example, when we remodeled our kitchen via 203K, we had to setup another kitchen area in our upstairs bonus room so that we could cook our meals. At times this will be frustrating but trust me; it'll all be worth it. The goal is to prepare yourself by asking "how can we plan ahead now to minimize comprises in our life as we move forward"?

6) Prepare for the kids and pets. Think of how the construction will impact them. Do we have to move them around the house? Should we make special provisions? Is it possible to find another home or location for them during the hours of construction activity? How can we keep them out of the way of the workers and away from dust, noise, paint or dirt?
The picture below is what you don't want to see! Keep Toto away from the work area…

7) Have a fist aid kit. It's a good idea to have a first aid kit handy in the event of injury.

8) Plan realistic solutions for bathrooms and kitchens that may be out of service. Like I mentioned earlier, if you have a kitchen or bathroom that will be out of service, you will need to plan accordingly. Setup a temporary kitchen area, create a schedule/rules for your family to use the other bathroom. Planning will help you tremendously.

9) Store delicate and profitable belonging. This sounds obvious, but it's amazing how many homeowners leave these kinds of things right out in the open, just begging to be broken or stolen. Don't take the chance, pack these things safety away!

10) Plan for dust and residue. Cover up electronics, furniture, and other valuable objects that aren't going to be removed from the construction area. You also should seal the doorways and vents. Change out your AC filters periodically and after the construction is over. Talk with you contractor about how they're going to keep sawdust, drywall dust, and other airborne contaminants under control.

11) Consider the impact of your project on your neighbors. There will be contractors, trucks, and construction equipment coming and going, as well as all the noise and mess they make. This may cause an inconvenience to your neighbors. Reach out to your neighbors and make them aware of what's coming up and let them know that you're going to do your best to make sure it doesn't negatively impact them. Encourage them to reach out to you directly at any time if there are any issues or concerns.

12) Plan some time away from the combat zone. Remodeling your home can sometimes be stressful and all the craziness can overwhelm your life. Schedule a few days away here and there to break up the insanity. This will give you some time to relax and refresh.

13) Demonstrate patience and realize the renovation is going to take longer than you'd like. Yup, said this before, but I thought I would repeat it again, so it can sink in.

SURVIVING THE CONTRACTORS

My next tips have to do with the day to day interaction with the contractors. The goal is to end up with a completed home that you've always wanted, yet with no pressure, viciousness, or gore over issues with the contractors.

Tips

- Do your due diligence. When choosing a contractor, make sure you determine whether they have a good track record and a good reputation. Ask around and look at reviews.

- Remember that builders are people too. Contractors have lives, families, and other commitments just like you. Their sole purpose isn't to work on your project. Also, most of them take pride in what they do, and even though they may not have graduated from business school or hold any professional degrees, they deserve our respect for their skills and experience.

- Show kindness and patience. Some people feel as though the only way things will get done is to take charge of the construction project and that intimidation and being demanding will give them greater control over the situation. However, most of the good contractors will not respond well to that kind of tactic. Remember, a little kindness can go a long way.

- Don't allow the contractors to push you around. At the same time we're showing contractors respect and patience, it's important that we receive the same back from them. If someone steps over the line into disrespectful communication or behavior, you will need to make it clear that this is not acceptable to you under any circumstances.

- Communication. Up front you need to have a clear understanding with the Contractor what the proper channels of communication are, how you will track things in writing, how you will finalize selections, changes and other matters. Eliminate the "he said she said." Document all changes, use your write up from your HUD consultant as a guide/blueprint of the work that needs to be done. Constantly get timelines from your contractor so that they will stay on schedule. Do not let weeks to go by without any work being done. Remember the work has to be completed within 6 months.

- Promises must be kept. We expect the contractors and others to keep their promises. We expect them to follow through with what they say they're going to do, so it's important that we do the same. Whether it's finalizing selections, visiting Home Depot or Lowes, processing documents.

for payment, have the dog kenneled, or other activities related to the project. Your actions can also hold up the progress so be mindful of this and stay on top of your duties and promises.

- Stay out of the way. You may get the urge to want to help out, stand around and visit, hold the ends of the boards, and find ways to be part of the fun. Unfortunately, most of the times all you're doing is slowing down the process. The best thing you can do is get out the way and let them work.

- Make notes of your questions or ideas. You will come up with questions and ideas so write them down so that you can present them to your Contractor. When you talk to your Contractor you can just go down the list at that time, otherwise you'll be calling and texting them every day. The more you stay organized the better for everyone.

- Make decisions promptly and on time. Try not to hold up the progress just because you can't decide on colors or other selections necessary to keep the project moving.

- Don't keep making changes. Try to make well thought-out decisions up front. In the case of a renovation loan, this is even more critical since processing changes to the scope of the work can cause issues for the lender relative to the funds in escrow, the appraisal value and other considerations.

 **Surviving the Construction Zone**

Here are some questions that you will need to ask in order to survive the construction zone!

1. Who is in charge of controlling dust and cleaning up the messes?
2. Who will put plastic up on entryways, cover vents, and so forth?
3. Who will cover furniture and other valuables?
4. Are there areas of the home that will be off limits or must be only accessed with special permission?
5. Is there a restroom in the house that is accessible for use by the laborers, or would it be a good idea to have a porta potty accommodated that reason?
6. What days and hours are sensible for work?
7. How early would we be able to have somebody there utilizing a cutting tool or making lots of noise and how late around evening time is that going to be acceptable?
8. Where will tools and materials be kept?
9. Where will brushes and containers be cleaned?
10. Should we anticipate dangerous fumes or odors?
11. Are there any occasions we should plan to go out for a couple of days?
12. How will the landscaping and grass be protected?
13. Who's responsible if damage to the driveway or the landscaping occurs?
14. How will interior items such as furniture, flooring, cabinets and appliances be protected and who will be responsible for any damage that may occur?
15. Who will be responsible for unlocking and locking the house when you're not there?
16. Who will provide advance notice on turning off the water, the power, the heat or other conveniences?
17. Where will the workers park?
18. Where will deliveries be made?
19. Is loud music and profanity on the jobsite expected or considered acceptable?
20. Will there be a dumpster?
21. When does the city pick up large debris from your neighborhood?

Now here are a couple of checklists that will help you with finding the right home to do a 203K loan.

Potential Home Checklist

Print out a few copies of this checklist to use as you visit prospective homes.
Having a record of what each home offers can make your final decision much easier.

Date Seen_____
Address_____Price_____Property Taxes_____
Seller_____Age of Home_____Neighborhood_____

Style of home ☐ Two Story ☐ Ranch ☐ Split Level ☐ Traditional ☐ Contemporary
               ☐ Cape cod   ☐ Townhouse ☐ Condo

Type of construction ☐ Wood ☐ Brick ☐ Stone ☐ Stucco ☐ Vinyl Siding ☐ Aluminum Siding

Exterior Features

Landscaping	☐ Good	☐ Fair	☐ Poor	
Fencing	☐ Good	☐ Fair	☐ Poor	☐ Nonexistent
Porch	☐ Good	☐ Fair	☐ Poor	☐ Nonexistent
Paint	☐ Good	☐ Fair	☐ Poor	
Patio	☐ Good	☐ Fair	☐ Poor	☐ Nonexistent
Deck	☐ Good	☐ Fair	☐ Poor	☐ Nonexistent
Garage	☐ 1 car	☐ 2 car	☐ 3 car	☐ Detached
	☐ Good	☐ Fair	☐ Poor	
Roof Condition	☐ Good	☐ Fair	☐ Poor	
Sidewalks	☐ Yes	☐ No		
Well-maintained neighborhood	☐ Yes	☐ No		

Interior Features

Kitchen Size_____
Eat-in ☐ Yes ☐ No
Flooring ☐ Ceramic ☐ Vinyl ☐ Wood ☐ Carpet ☐ Good ☐ Fair ☐ Poor
Appliances ☐ Good ☐ Fair ☐ Poor ☐ Nonexistent
Cabinets ☐ Good ☐ Fair ☐ Poor
Windows ☐ Good ☐ Fair ☐ Poor

Dining room Size_____
Flooring ☐ Carpet ☐ Hardwood ☐ Tile ☐ Good ☐ Fair ☐ Poor
Lighting fixtures ☐ Good ☐ Fair ☐ Poor ☐ Nonexistent

Living room Size_____
Flooring ☐ Carpet ☐ Hardwood ☐ Tile ☐ Good ☐ Fair ☐ Poor
Lighting fixtures ☐ Good ☐ Fair ☐ Poor ☐ Nonexistent
Fireplace ☐ Good ☐ Fair ☐ Poor ☐ Nonexistent

Den Size_____
Flooring ☐ Carpet ☐ Hardwood ☐ Tile ☐ Good ☐ Fair ☐ Poor
Lighting fixtures ☐ Good ☐ Fair ☐ Poor ☐ Nonexistent
Fireplace ☐ Good ☐ Fair ☐ Poor ☐ Nonexistent

Hallway
Flooring ☐ Carpet ☐ Hardwood ☐ Tile ☐ Good ☐ Fair ☐ Poor
Linen closet ☐ Good ☐ Fair ☐ Poor ☐ Nonexistent

Total bedrooms_____
Bedroom 1	Size_____						
	Flooring	☐Carpet	☐Hardwood	☐Tile	☐Good	☐Fair	☐Poor
	Closet	☐Good	☐Fair	☐Poor	☐Nonexistent		

Bedroom 2	Size_____						
	Flooring	☐Carpet	☐Hardwood	☐Tile	☐Good	☐Fair	☐Poor
	Closet	☐Good	☐Fair	☐Poor	☐Nonexistent		

Bedroom 3	Size_____						
	Flooring	☐Carpet	☐Hardwood	☐Tile	☐Good	☐Fair	☐Poor
	Closet	☐Good	☐Fair	☐Poor	☐Nonexistent		

Total Bathrooms_____
Master Bath	Size_____						
	Flooring	☐Ceramic	☐Vinyl	☐Wood	☐Carpet	☐Good	☐Fair ☐Poor
	Tub	☐Good	☐Fair	☐Poor			
	Fixtures	☐Good	☐0Fair	☐Poor			

Guest Bath	Size_____						
	Flooring	☐Ceramic	☐Vinyl	☐Wood	☐Carpet	☐Good	☐Fair ☐Poor
	Tub	☐Good	☐Fair	☐Poor			
	Fixtures	☐Good	☐Fair	☐Poor			

Laundry room	Location_____			
	Washer	☐Good	☐Fair	☐Poor	☐Nonexistent
	Dryer	☐Good	☐Fair	☐Poor	☐Nonexistent

Good closet space ☐Yes ☐No

Basement ☐Yes ☐No ☐Finished ☐Carpet ☐Hardwood ☐Tile

Utilities

Type of heating	☐Hot water	☐Gas	☐Electric	☐Oil
Insulation	☐Fiberglass	☐Cellulose	☐Foam	☐Nonexistent
Central Air	☐Yes	☐No		
Plumbing Condition	☐Good	☐Fair	☐Poor	
Sump pump/drainage system		☐Yes	☐No	
Connected to sewer system		☐Yes	☐No	

Age of heating system_____
Age/capacity of water heater_____
Age of electrical wiring_____

Easy proximity to:
☐Work ☐Schools ☐Shopping ☐Airport Area ☐Industry ☐Highways
☐Houses of worship ☐Train station ☐Public transportation ☐Doctors/dentists

Recent sales in neighborhood:
Address_____Size_____Price_____
Address_____Size_____Price_____
Address_____Size_____Price_____
Address_____Size_____Price_____

Renovation Checklist

Duplicate this page for use as you inspect prospective homes for improvements needed.

Address_____

Room/Location	Problem Area	Renovation Needed

I hope that you have enjoyed this eBook!

Thanks to the 203k Loan, my wife and I were able to turn an older outdated house into the home of our dreams!! **We accomplished this without coming out of pocket for renovations upfront or getting a separate loan for remodeling.** By reading this eBook you now have the knowledge to do the same. I believe a 203k loan is the best resource to help people update older homes. My mission is to spread the news about this opportunity! I've put all the good and the not so good that we've learned throughout this 203k process inside of this eBook and I'm confident that if you follow all the principles in this book you will have a successful 203k experience. Move over Chip and Joanna, now it's time for you to do your Fixer Upper! Happy House Hunting and Happy Remodeling!

Here are some real-life success stories of 203K loans

Purchase Price: $177,075
Appraised value after completion: $215,000
Total Rehab: $21,000.00
Repairs/Improvements:
- Foundation Repair
- Insulation
- Repair Exterior Cracks and Rotting Wood
- Replace Shutters

Purchase Price: $135,401.00
Appraised value after completion: $210,000.00
Total Rehab: $61,556.40
Repairs/Improvements:
New Roof
Landscaping
- Flooring
- Bathroom Renovation
- Kitchen Appliances & cabinets
- Foundation Repair

Purchase Price: $120,000.00

Appraised Value After Completion: $220,000.00

Total Rehab: $82,263.50

Closed "As Is" With These Issues:

- Cracked exterior brick
- Electrical not up to code
- HVAC not working
- Termite damage
- Damaged siding

Purchase Price: $226,000.00

Appraised value after completion: $305,000.00

Total Rehab: $56,643.50

Closed "As Is" With These Issues:

- Master bath missing all fixtures and plumbing was damaged
- Septic System was not functioning
- Electrical system not up to code
- No appliances in kitchen

Repairs/Improvements:

- Installed new carpet & updated granite in kitchen
- Replaced septic system
- Installed new appliances in kitchen
- Upgraded electrical system and installed new lighting fixtures

Purchase Price: $111,000.00

Appraised value after completion: $265,000.00

Total Rehab: $54,200.00

Closed "As Is" With These Issues:

- Missing windows
- Damaged HVAC
- Out of date electrical system
- Foundation issues

Repairs/Improvements:

- Replaced all doors and windows
- Repaired sheetrock and foundation
- Replaced HVAC, appliances, and cabinets

Purchase Price: $135,182.00

Appraised value after completion: $190,000.00

Total Rehab: $28,482.00

Closed "As Is" with these issues:

- House had mold issues
- Foundation problems
- Pool needed cleaning and fence around pool was damaged
- Plumbing not up to code and missing fixtures throughout house

Repairs/Improvements:

Cleaned mold and completed air quality testing

- Repaired foundation, interior wall damage, and painted entire house
- Installed new plumbing, hot water heater, and fixtures

Copyright Notice & Legal Notice
©Nation Home Services
256.337.3238 Nation Home Services is a division of QRES, LLC.

All rights reserved. While attempts have been made to verify information provided in this publication, neither the author nor the publisher assumes any responsibility for errors, omissions, or contradictory information contained in this document. This document is not intended as legal, accounting or investment advice. The reader of this document assumes all responsibility for the use of these materials and information.

Made in the USA
Las Vegas, NV
01 December 2023

81950588R00024